MERCEDES SOSA
Voice of the People

Aixa Pérez-Prado

Children's Book Press
An imprint of LEE & LOW BOOKS INC.
New York

Have you ever heard a song that made your heart soar?

A canción that captured your corazón?

A voice so powerful that it made you feel ready to change the world?

This is the story of a singer whose voice sailed through the air like the wings of a condor, inspiring people everywhere.

Mercedes Sosa was born on July 9, 1935, in Tucumán, Argentina. It was Independence Day, and a 21-gun salute heralded her arrival.

From a young age, Mercedes sang in her home, at her school, at celebrations, and even in the cemetery. When people heard her, their hands raised in applause, and their hearts rose with esperanza.

Her powerful voice carried the colors of the cordillera and the pulse of the pampas.

Mercedes's family was a duet of Indigenous
and European ancestry. In her humble home,
sometimes there was not enough to eat, but there was
always an abundance of amor.

One day Mercedes and her brother Chichi snuck into a sugar
mill to watch their father work. Their papá was in charge of
keeping the hungry furnace lit.

The furnace breathed fire and soot. Papá lifted his shovel
over and over again to feed it. Mercedes watched her father
sweat, struggle, and strain. All for a few pesos to feed
his family.

She never forgot that day.

When Mercedes was a teenager, her parents traveled to Buenos Aires to celebrate Peronist Loyalty Day. President Perón's populist party promised better jobs for the working poor.

While her parents were away, friends convinced Mercedes to enter a singing contest at a local radio station. She knew her father would not approve, but she entered the contest anyway under a false name: "Gladys Osorio."

And to her surprise, Mercedes won!

The radio station asked her to sing on air every afternoon. Mercedes's voice yearned to fly, so she snuck out to sing without her father's permission.

One afternoon, Don Ernesto heard a familiar voice coming from the radio and immediately recognized it as his daughter's.

Her secret was revealed!

Papá was angry, but Mamá convinced him to let Mercedes keep singing on air. Doña Ema knew her daughter's voice was meant to soar.

When she was twenty-two years old, Mercedes married guitarist and composer Oscar Matus. At the time, folklore Argentino, the traditional music of the people, was being forgotten, but Oscar was determined to give it new life.

Mercedes and Oscar became active members of the Nuevo Cancionero movement, which championed social justice through music. Inspired by folklore Argentino, this movement used indigenous sounds and instruments, reimagining them in new ways.

Together Mercedes and Oscar sang, strummed, and drummed from Tucumán to Mendoza to the capital, Buenos Aires.

Their harmonies carried the indigenous rhythms and instruments of el pueblo. Their lyrics spoke of poverty, libertad, and love for all people—echoing what Mercedes believed in her heart.

When Oscar and Mercedes's marriage crumbled and the duo disbanded, Mercedes's heart sank. With a son to care for, she had to find the strength to fly solo.

And keep cantando.

Through the following years, Mercedes made friends with poets, painters, musicians, and thinkers. They encouraged her to continue using her voice for social change. Her songs spoke about heartache and healing, love and loss. She sang about the unfairness of poverty and inequality in the world.

Mercedes performed in concerts and festivals throughout Latin America, and, later, Europe and the United States.

Her music delivered messages of unity, hope, and empowerment. It motivated people to stand up against injustice and to confront oppressors. Her singing helped poor and Indigenous people feel seen and heard, lifting and giving courage to their corazones.

Mercedes gave a voice to the voiceless.

But some powerful people in Argentina wanted to clip Mercedes's wings. Why would songs that inspired hope and courage make them so angry?

Argentina was ruled by a military junta from 1976 to 1983. Thousands of Argentines, accused of working against the government, were taken to secret locations, interrogated, and tortured. Some never returned. They were known as "los desaparecidos." Women who gave birth in custody had their babies given to strangers, shattering families beyond repair.

It was a dark period in the history of Argentina known as La Guerra Sucia—The Dirty War.

While many artists fled the country for safety, Mercedes kept singing songs of resistance. The songs were considered dangerous by the junta. Many were banned from the radio, and some of her shows were shut down. When her life was threatened, friends urged her to leave Argentina.

In 1979 at a concert in La Plata, soldiers stormed the stage. Mercedes was arrested and the entire audience was detained.

Fearing for her safety, Mercedes reluctantly went into exile in France and later Spain, leaving her family and country behind.

For three years, the wind whisked Mercedes's melodies from Europe over the wide sea to Argentina, lifting the corazones of her gente.

While living in exile, she became known as La Voz de Latinoamérica.

más lejos del hogar estas,

más cerca del corazón lo llevas

In 1982, wearing her international fame as armor, Mercedes returned to Argentina. Her heart pounded in her chest like the beat of a bombo as a customs officer examined her passport, tracing Mercedes's time in exile. Then he told her what she dreaded most to hear: she did not have permission to enter Argentina.

Mercedes took a deep breath and declared her right to enter the country as an Argentine citizen. The officer looked Mercedes in the eyes and said nothing. Mercedes refused to move. After a long pause, the officer stamped her passport and allowed her to pass.

Mercedes was finally home, but would the people welcome her back?

Outside, Mercedes was met by cheering fans and signs of bienvenida. As she reached the city center, crowds of people gathered along her path.

Argentina welcomed her with arms spread as wide as condor wings.

At her first concert since exile, Mercedes sensed the entusiasmo in the air. When she stepped on stage, the audience erupted in applause, crying and chanting her name.

Mercedes closed her eyes and savored the moment.

Then her strong voice rang out.

Yo tengo tantos hermanos . . .

But the junta was not happy with Mercedes's return. They feared that her powerful voice would inspire even more resistance from activists already fighting for human rights in Argentina.

One group, Las Madres, mothers of desaparecidos, demanded the truth about their missing children. Their weekly demonstrations at the Plaza de Mayo caught the attention of other nations.

At the same time, a failed military campaign added further conflict within the regime. The junta's hold on the country loosened, cracked, and finally collapsed in 1983.

The dictatorship was over.

As a sense of peace and freedom returned to Argentina, Mercedes's uplifting songs of empathy and esperanza, fearlessness and fuerza helped the country begin to heal. For the rest of her life, Mercedes spoke up for the rights of all people and the environment.

Even today her songs live on, and her voice continues to inspire.

Have you ever heard a song that made your heart soar?

A canción that captured your corazón?

Afterword

Born to Be Free

Mercedes Sosa was born on Argentine Independence Day—July 9, 1935—in the province of Tucumán. It is the smallest province in Argentina, located in the northwest of the country. She grew up in a modest and happy home with siblings and a loving family of French, Spanish, and Indigenous ancestry. Her parents, Ema and Ernesto, worked as a washerwoman and a laborer. She credited them with keeping their family rich with love despite living in poverty. Mercedes often remembered that on Saturdays when her father got paid, her mother would make them noodles with butter. Sometimes it was the only hot meal they had all week. When there was nothing to eat, her mother would take the children to play in a nearby park at mealtimes so they wouldn't smell other people's food. As a child and teen, Mercedes loved to sing and dance. She later learned to play the bombo, an indigenous drum, as well as the guitar, piano, and charango. Although she never wrote her own music, many musicians asked her to sing their songs, some writing with her voice in mind. Her version of songs such as "Solo le pido a Dios" by León Greco and "Alfonsina y el mar" by Félix Luna and Ariel Ramirez made them iconic.

A Woman of Many Names

Born Haydée Mercedes Sosa, she was called Marta by her family and friends. She began her career after winning a singing contest under the name "Gladys Osorio" in an attempt to keep her participation hidden from her disapproving parents. She was eventually called Mercedes professionally, then given the nickname La Negra—"The Black One"—by her fans. In Argentina, many people of

Mercedes Sosa 1960s

mixed and Indigenous ancestry, or people with dark hair, are referred to as "Negro/a." Mercedes adopted and embraced this nickname, which emphasized her Indigenous roots. Later, she was called the Voice of Latin America and the Mother of Latin America by many who credited her with being a powerful voice who used music and song to fight for freedom and justice.

A New Voice

Mercedes and her husband, Manuel Oscar Matus, became important players in the Nuevo Cancionero movement in Argentina, which stated as its goal that songs should come from the common people and that music should exist to speak the truth without fear. The music was inspired by the many Indigenous and rural people who began to flood the big cities in the 1960s and 1970s as the poverty in rural areas was so great that they could not survive. The struggles and repression they faced were fundamental to the social movement that became associated with the music. As part of the Nuevo Cancionero movement, Mercedes began to be censored by authorities who did not like her message of social justice. Other important musicians who were part of this movement included Armando Tejada Gómez and Tito Francia.

Loneliness and Depression

Although Mercedes had a successful career as an artist and was a loving mother to son Fabián Matus, she sometimes suffered from anxiety and depression. After Oscar left her, she felt abandoned and struggled financially. She started borrowing money from friends and drinking heavily. However, once she realized how alcohol was affecting her, she stopped drinking. Mercedes credited her partner Pocho Mazzitelli with helping her career blossom again. When he passed away, she felt a profound loss that accompanied her throughout her life. In later life, she suffered further bouts of depression and spent several months in bed at one point. With the help of prayers and well wishes from her fans, friends, and family; medication; and treatment by doctors, Mercedes got back on her feet.

Fear and Courage

During the 1970s, Argentina was plagued with political instability, a high rate of inflation, unemployment, and debt. Many people were struggling to make a living, and there was a feeling of unrest in the country. The military wanted to restore order, and, in 1976, a junta led by General Jorge Videla came to power. During what is now commonly known as the Dirty War—a term considered problematic, as the events described involve state-sponsored terrorism

rather than a traditional war—the government targeted people who were seen as a threat to its power. It's estimated that around thirty thousand people "disappeared" during this time. These disappearances involved torture, imprisonment, and even killings.

Mercedes Sosa received anonymous letters telling her to leave the country for her own good. Her music was banned from many radio stations, and places she performed were threatened with closure. Finally, at a concert in La Plata in 1979, she was arrested on stage by military police after singing a prohibited song that talked of injustice by the military. The song was "La carta" by Violeta Parra. Mercedes's son, Fabián, and the entire audience were also detained. International pressure by fans led to Mercedes's quick release. Still, she did not want to leave Argentina and continued trying to perform. However, after several more occasions where her shows were canceled and she felt threatened, Mercedes finally decided to go into exile. She moved to Paris and later Madrid, where she could continue to sing without fear. She was well received in other European countries, and her international fame grew during this time. But, Mercedes longed to return to Argentina.

Mercedes with the bombo,
a traditional drum used in Argentine folklore.

The Return of Hope

Mercedes returned to Argentina in 1982, shortly before the military dictatorship collapsed. The Argentine public welcomed her with great enthusiasm and excitement. Her return inspired hope and courage in other musicians and artists. Mercedes continued to sing her songs of protest and social justice as well as to expand her repertoire. She began to perform with many other musicians, who sang different styles of music, including rock, jazz, pop, and hip-hop. Her son, Fabián Matus, introduced her to new and upcoming singers with varied musical styles. Mercedes performed with Joan Baez, Andrea Bocelli, Charly García, León Gieco, René Pérez, Carlos Santana, Shakira, and Sting, among others. She was always looking for new kinds of music and ways to express herself through song and was always supportive of young and upcoming artists.

Honors and Awards

Throughout her life, Mercedes performed in many countries and in many prestigious locations, including Carnegie Hall and the Vatican. She won several Latin Grammy awards, as well as the Konex Platinum Award for Best Female Folklore Singer and the Konex Brilliant Award for Best Popular Artist of the Decade. She also received various awards for her music and activism from countries including Peru, Brazil, and Ecuador. In 1996 she received the Conseil International de la Musique–UNESCO award. This award is given to musicians whose work contributes to peace and international cooperation through music. The jury noted that they were giving Mercedes this honor not only for her brilliant career but also in recognition of her continuous defense of human rights in Argentina, even during the darkest times of its dictatorship. Mercedes became the UNESCO Goodwill Ambassador for Latin America and the Caribbean. She said that this was the most important of the awards and honors she received in her lifetime because it allowed her to be a spokeswoman for children in need.

Glossary

amor—love
bienvenida—welcome
canción—song
cantando—singing
corazón—heart
cordillera—mountain range
desaparecidos—the disappeared

entusiasmo—enthusiasm
esperanza—hope
fuerza—strength
gente—people
libertad—freedom
pueblo—community
voz—voice

Bibliography

Almeida, H. L. *Mercedes Sosa: Voz de la zamba.* Buenos Aires: Editorial Biblos, 2005.

Braceli, Rodolfo. *Mercedes Sosa: La Negra.* Buenos Aires: Editorial Sudamericana, 2010.

———. "Mercedes Sosa, la Negra, la Marta." *Caras y Caretas*, September 30, 2019. https://carasycaretas.org.ar/2019/09/30/mercedes-sosa-la-negra-la-marta/.

Christensen, Anette. *Mercedes Sosa, the Voice of Hope: My Life-Transforming Encounter.* Tribute2Life Publishing, 2019.

Espinosa, Roberto. *Mercedes Sosa, una canción en el viento.* Tucumán, Argentina: Editorial Ciudad Histórica San Miguel de Tucumán, 2020.

Fundación Mercedes Sosa. "Biografía." Fundación Mercedes Sosa, August 4, 2019. https://www.mercedessosa.org/biografia/.

Heckman, Don. "The Voice Heard Round the World: Mercedes Sosa, a Compelling Figure in World Music and Social Activist, Will Make a Rare L.A. Appearance." October 29, 1995. https://www.latimes.com/archives/la-xpm-1995-10-29-ca-62462-story.html.

Jalil, V. *Mercedes Sosa Para Chic@s.* Buenos Aires: Editorial Sudestada, 2016.

Luna, Félix. *Mercedes Sosa: La Voz de América.* Buenos Aires: Editorial Sudamericana, 2014.

Menéndez, J., and I. C. Mendoza. *Latinitas: Una celebración de 40 soñadoras audaces.* New York: Godwin Books, Henry Holt and Company, 2022.

"Mercedes Sosa, la voz de la canción protesta latinoamericana, muere a los 74 años." *El País*, October 5, 2009.

Roberts, S. B. "Mercedes Sosa: The Singer Who Gave Voice to Her People's Struggle Outlived Several Tyrants." *Plough*, June 14, 2012. https://www.plough.com/en/topics/culture/music/mercedes-sosa.

Rohter, L. "Mercedes Sosa: A Voice of Hope." *The New York Times*, October 9, 1988.

Rojas, Eduardo Marceles. *La Negra Mercedes: El canto popular argentino.* Buenos Aires: Ediciones Corregidor, 2012.

Vila, Rodrigo, dir. *Mercedes Sosa: La Voz de Latinoamérica.* 2013; Buenos Aires: Cinema 7 Films.

Willachur, Ricardo, dir. *Mercedes Sosa: Como un pájaro libre.* 1983; Buenos Aires: Emerald.

Para Salta 760, 3° B, y todo lo que fue y siempre será para mí.
Y para Abuela Fé, la cantora que lo convirtió en hogar.
—A. P.-P.

Pages 24–25 "más lejos del hogar . . .": Translated from the English. Hernandez, Sandra. "Sosa's Land Always Near in Her Songs." *South Florida Sun Sentinel*, September 24, 2003.

Page 36 photo: Mercedes Sosa: La "Negra" y su bombo, 1962. Photograph by Annemarie Heinrich, courtesy of Wikimedia Commons.

Page 37 photo: Musica Foklorica Argentina, Mercedes Sosa accompanies herself on a drum, 1967. Photo collection Anefo, courtesy of National Archives, CC0, Netherlands.

Children's Book Press, *an imprint of* LEE & LOW BOOKS INC.
95 Madison Avenue
New York, NY 10016
leeandlow.com

Edited by Jessica V. Echeverria
Book design by Ashley Halsey
Book production by The Kids at Our House
The text is set in Weidemann Std
The illustrations are digital collage
Manufactured in China by Toppan
10 9 8 7 6 5 4 3 2 1
First Edition

Library of Congress Cataloging-in-Publication Data
Names: Pérez-Prado, Aixa, author, illustrator.
Title: Mercedes Sosa : voice of the people / by Aixa Pérez-Prado.
Description: First edition. | New York : Children's Book Press, an imprint of Lee & Low Books, Inc., 2024. |
Audience: Ages 7–13 (provided by Children's Book Press)
Identifiers: LCCN 2023043698 | ISBN 9780892394708 (hardcover) | ISBN 9780892394715 (ebk)
Subjects: LCSH: Sosa, Mercedes—Juvenile literature. | Singers—Argentina—Biography—Juvenile literature. |
LCGFT: Biographies. | Picture books.
Classification: LCC ML3930.S686 P37 2024 | DDC 782.4216492 [B 23'eng'20230]—dc20
LC record available at https://lccn.loc.gov/2023043698